Rebellious Ideas

Rebellious Ideas

Shehu Sani

authorHOUSE®

AuthorHouse™
1663 Liberty Drive
Bloomington, IN 47403
www.authorhouse.com
Phone: 1-800-839-8640

Published by AuthorHouse   04/08/2013

ISBN: 978-1-4817-8982-0 (sc)

Author's Note

The human brain and mind is a factory of ideas. It's a source and a fountain of thoughts. Constructive and destructive ideas. Positive and evil thoughts. Its where the seed of war is sown and where the harvest of peace begins. In thoughts, humanity elevates its status and advances its knowledge. Ideas and thoughts influences the lives of men and shape the destiny of humanity.

The world of today evolves from the world of yesterday, but its different in its level of organisation and anarchy. The world of tomorrow will evolve from that of today and will characteristically be different. Philosophical, ideological and sociological thoughts that could turn out to be realistic, factual and pragmatic today can dissolve in the truth of the changing times. There are however some times that defy the vacillations and fluctuations of times and changing realities.

Knowledge is infinite and so is ignorance. There will never be a time when there is nothing new to learn. Every civilization will be met with its realities and challenges; some it inherits and other it emerges. Man lives in constant conflicts with the issues of his time. Answers are found by seeking out solutions through ideas and thoughts that constitutes the subject matter.

A human being is born free and unhinded but later assume identities as a husband, a citizen, a lawyer, a cleric a politician or a musician. What you become may not be what you wanted to be, but what you are becomes your destiny. In man's journey to become, he learns, he tries, he fails, he rises, he gets inspired. And there are always inhibitions and impediments; mischief, betrayal, disappointments, opposition, incapacities and limitations. Everyone differs in his or her responses to what we see, meet or feel in life. Some are persistent, some give up easily, some feel challenged, some feel defeated.

Millions of books have been written and history has produced the best in motivation and inspiration. Humans influence each other by the life we live or the word we utter, our lives is a bit of the lives of others, knowingly or unknowingly.

There is power in speech and writing born out of great ideas and atimes destructive ones. The oppressed have in history found freedom through inspirational speeches and literary intervention.

Rebellious ideas combines the features of inspiration, motivation and idealism that touches on the political, social, spiritual, cultural, sociological aspects of the individual and the collective; his essences, his soul, his place and his relationship with his immediate and larger society. These ideas are arrows that aim at or target aspects of man's life that concerns his person, his personal and his society.

Rebellious ideas are meant to challenge existing norms and beliefs but in some cases strengthen them. The book is primarily aimed at stimulating thoughts by laying facts and truth bare in a manner that is short and straight to the point.

In a busy world and in a world where people have more than enough to read, rebellious ideas is adapted to find a space in readership and in thoughts. Rebellious ideas is about the life we live. It addresses our soul, our conscience. It is indeed intended to stimulate and provoke a wave of reaction.

Dedication

To my father Sani Hassan

Acknowledgement

I wish to acknowledge the mystery, the magic and resourcefulness that is characteristic of our turbulent and troubled times. I wish to appreciate the patience and understanding of my family. And Mr. Cole Michaels who compiled these thoughts and Felicia who type set them and Ibrahim Baba who supervises the process have all done a good job for posterity.

Politics

A bad decision needs a reversal no matter how late.

A building is a collective product of diverse skills and profession.

A change is a current.

A Chinese phone can never be cowed to silence.

A cleric who claims to know about evil spirits, cannot claim ignorance about their human counterparts.

A corrupt Government personalizes the treasury of the state.

A corrupt state bores and exhaust.

A democratic Government learn to live with the irritating truth of a free press and a tyranny rise against it.

A divided opposition, a perpetual Government.

A fisherman whose net catches both fishes and snakes, must learn the art of separating them.

A free society cannot question your beliefs but can question your action,

A free society cannot question your beliefs but can question your action.

A freeman think a prisoner lost his freedom, a prisoner think a freeman knew not the value of freedom.

A frozen justice can only be warmed by the heat of a protest.

A functional state insures the led against decadence and the leaders against tragedy.

A government cannot do anything outside of its mission in power, including looting and lies.

A Government not felt in our lives is a government absent in our lives.

A Government not in the service of the people is in the service of itself.

A Government of the few can only be appreciated by the few.

A Government that bows to the will of its people has bowed to the essence of its existence.

A government that derails do same as a train that derails.

A Government that do not listen to the voice of its people, should feel the fists of its people.

A Government that has run out of ideas, has run out of steam.

A government that have no honour in its stock cannot dispense it to others.

A Government voted for its promise should be rated by its fulfillment.

A honest king who died poor, lives behind a good name and a grumbling wife.

A king is a prisoner with power.

A leader disconnected from his people must chose his route of presence.

A leader not prepared for power, will always need more time in power.

A leader who has nothing to deliver, needs no time to deliver it.

A leader who must give much for friends will give crumbs to the people.

A leader who plant a tree and Quit is more appreciated than the one who gives a fruit and over stay.

A man with stolen gloves can't fight corruption.

A menace grows from a little seed of ignored wrong.

A Nation grows and out grows from the mentality of its founding fathers.

A nation like a building fails from the pillars.

A Nation that cannot live up to our collective dream, should not take away our individual sleep.

A Nation that imports its food imports its appetite.

A nation that kills the dreams of its citizens, halts its advance forward.

A nation that waste talents, emits the highest of carbon.

A nation where survival is the first order of its people, is a nation in need of rescue.

A Nation's wealth in the hands of a few is a Nation's throat on the grip of a few.

A parliament dominated by young people is a party hall.

A people in protest is a power in motion.

A politician library is stuffed with unread books.

A probe not implemented is a study.

A Queen doesn't see the king in her man, she sees a husband.

A regime rots from the root.

A rogue leadership elevates their family to the state and degrades the state to their family.

A Ruler who was uses the name of God to steal, will get a helping hand from the men of God.

A stampede on the treasury of a nation suffocates its people.

A state that killed its people is a state on death row.

A super minister is a minister that cannot be removed by popular disgust.

A surrender is not a defeat but an acceptance that you have won for now.

A thieving government destroys not just a state, but a generation.

A throne of power is carved of thorns and not of roses.

A tree can make a forest if that tree stands for justice.

All dogs in homes and in palaces are deployed to bark.

All men of conscience, owe it a duty to raise the shield of freedom against the sword of fear.

America and the west broke the Dam of communism and it's now suffering the flood.

An election funded by rogues brings a Government run by rogues.

An impotent opposition, an enduring tyranny.

An organized state treasures its history and work for its future.

An uninspiring leader kills the spirit of a nation.

Any destructive government want constructive criticism.

As a nation, we will overcome this orgy.

As the world economic pendulum swings to the east, shouldn't we all start learning Chinese language?

Avoid the Dog that barks, dread the one that don't.

Because of money, the harmony between the rich and the poor sits on acrimony.

Before a jail break comes a law break.

Before abusing office, conscience is abused first.

Before you raise the Hand of a candidate in the public, make sure he has a clean armpit.

Behind the corporate world is the corporate crime.

Betrayal is heinous in life and in politics its life.

Big Ben is heard by people who have never met it.

Brutal regimes and idolatry deities need spill blood to survive.

By indifference or silence, you share the collective guilt of your generation,

Capital alone cannot make a business without the Habits of a Trader.

Captain of industry without an industry becomes an industry of captains.

Clean politics is like a clean toilet, you still can't eat there.

Corruption can't be exorcised from a system that formally endorses class inequality and inequity.

Crisis test are resolve, prolong crisis tests our resilience.

Critics pull down a Government, praise singers pulls down a nation.

Defecating in an open field is freedom of expression.

Democracy is majority resolve for the common good and individual choice.

Diversification, is the film that made Nollywood actresses richer than the actors.

Donating stolen money for religious causes is not called money laundering.

Double standard means there is no standing standard for a stand.

Dubai has shown that Rome can be built in a day.

Each day a journalist spend in jail is a day lost to tyranny.

Every choice of a leader is a worthy gamble or a misadventure.

Everyday for the Haves, one day for the Have not.

Every nation decides its fate by its conscience.

First the vote, then the responsibility, the legitimacy of a Government is established.

For a Government to exist, it must be present in your life.

Forbes can profile the wealth of men but not the state of their mind.

Free society embraces the beauty of diversity, not the evil of divisiveness.

Freedom and faith are of equal invincibility.

Freedom is a whole, there is no half democracy but half tyranny.

Freedom is like a toothpaste, once released out, can never be retrieved back.

Freedom is opportunity as much as it is rights.

Genuine Compassion to one needy person is compassion to the whole of humanity.

God want by your heart and justice need your voice.

Good luck can give a crown, not retain it.

Great nations are built upon great ideas.

Hardships are meant to generate ideas of invention or of revolt.

He who missed the tiger with the first spear, knows what to do.

Hear all, Listen to some.

Hostility towards the press is the first symptom of an ailing and failing Government.

I have no problem with your beliefs, if your beliefs denies not my right to my beliefs.

If a King must die to leave the Throne, then Throne is the Killer of the Kings.

If men and women are equal, why separate Toilets.

If murder is the road to heaven, you could not have been born.

If the King loves Black colour, some will brush with charcoal to prove their loyalty.

If the people cannot speak outdoors, they will plot indoors.

If there is one more message the Lord should send to mankind, is the book of interpretation.

If we all run away from a raging fire, it will eventually incinerate us all.

If you are close to the corridors of power, you will be used to false steps

If you are confident about your faith, you can talk to the devil.

If you are neither here nor there and ended up nowhere, you are a pendulum.

If you can fill a basket with water, you can build a nation with corruption.

If you chase a thief with a stolen shoe, both of you will be chased.

If you have an hour to speak about the things you know, you don't have to fill it up with the things you don't know.

If you have doubt about people knowing your secrets, join politics.

If you have to celebrate in heavy security, you are celebrating security.

If you hold a minority view, you are either right or mad.

If you remove money from politics, it becomes an idea.

If you swim to Europe in this hard times, you will need a life buoy to stay afloat.

If you talk a lot, people can't remember what you say.

If your Iris is made of your sentiment, that becomes your vision and view.

If your neigbours are all like you, you will have harmony and nothing new to learn.

In a Black Maria, you appreciate the beauty and freedom in trekking.

In a government of colours, a red situation has to wait for a white paper and a blue print.

In a highly criminalized state, public offices are crime scenes.

In a Land of entrenched inequity, philanthropy does not eradicate poverty.

In a parliament where Bills attract bills, conscience is on recess.

In a nation with short memory, the shoulders of tyrants are always high.

In dissent a nation assent.

In electoral politics, there is no silver and bronze medalists.

In places where people do not matter, its things that matter.

In politics, Judas is an inspiration.

In some nations, people tell their leaders to run. In some nations, leaders tell their people they will run.

In the guise of religion, you can fool all people all the time.

In the kitchen cabinet is where the oven is.

In tyranny and in religion, there are limits to question you can ask or get answers.

Insurgency undermines expression, expression undermine insurgency.

It's easy to stand ashore and tell a canoe passenger to fight the crocodile.

Its either a government chose to pillage or to reform, but it can't chose to pillage and reform.

Justice delayed is justice bought.

Justice delayed is justice purchased.

Justice without freedom is a Government justice. Freedom without justice is a Government freedom.

Lawyers defend you with their facts, not their heart.

Leaders preoccupied with protecting themselves, have little left to protect their people.

Leadership is a rare opportunity, to reveal your genius and unveil that of others.

Life traumatize the poor, death torments the rich.

Loot a state, kill its spirit.

Lower taste cures lower earnings.

Loyalists protect a ruler from the foes and the truth.

Mass protest is the most effective hearing aid for a deaf Government.

Monkeys have limited trusts and limited friends.

Nigeria, looted nation, raped people.

No Government borrows to pay within its tenure.

No government can survive a tenacious spirit of objection.

No matter your dictatorial tendencies, you can never silence a Chinese phone.

No nation can't address its questions and its woes by flushing them.

Nollywood film producers seriously believe in the dictum that what must go up, must come down.

Not all gathering of clouds leads to rain.

On the day of Jail Break, to stay behind or to run is dangerous.

On the day of protest, bring your body and your worries to the street.

On this Eid, we pray that may the permitted slaughter end all unpermitted slaughter.

One man of faith can stand an Army of duty.

Only a journalist can praise a Government without the media calling him a sycophant.

Only the Government of God can reach and administer the territory of the mind.

Only those who will move towards the fire, can rescue those already in the fire.

Only when a winner is honest in victory can a looser be graceful in defeat.

Our country have higher record of people honored for achievement than its recorded achievements.

Our country is an enduring but strange country that consistently disappoints her pessimists and prove wrong her optimists.

Our humanity is in our sanity.

Our individual achievements dissolves in the collective waste of our generation.

Parliamentarians whose hands are oily greased cannot lift the weight of responsibility.

Paying the electorate is buying air time.

People cannot be passionate about a dispassionate country.

People who are given a wide space to write, many feed their readers with space.

Political scandal is a nation's blockbuster.

Politics is the only industry that can absorb everybody.

Politics is the only profession you will enter alone and find your family in it.

Poverty and affluence have an equal capacity to influence the mind of Man.

Poverty undermines the exercise of all rights and freedoms.

Praise singers get the most in religion and in politics.

Progress stops where corruption begins.

Public figure means public scrutiny.

Public firms don't work until they are auctioned to public officers through their fronts.

Readmission extinguishes the flame of the disgruntled.

Real estate doesn't mean there isn't a fake one.

Revolution buries your anguish and grows your dream.

Rich king, poor subjects is King of the Poor.

Riot is a protest on auto pilot.

Rogue elites infest the society.

Silence in the midst of evil is conscience on the retreat.

Snakes moves freely in unattended bushes.

Some gifts are Handcuffs.

Stand for the truth or lay in lies.

Tear Gas is the fragrance of the protester.

The Army of unemployed are reservists for a revolution.

The art of saying good about the Government and the opposition at the same time is called objectivity in journalism.

The baton for a loyalist is to cover up tracks of mess and debt.

The best adviser the king needs is his conscience.

The capital city gives a false impression about a country.

The chain of tyranny enslaves the poor, the chain of unity frees the poor.

The communist china has silence everyone, except their phone.

The constitution is the citizens amendable scripture.

The disabled include the impoverished.

The goods market can't be safe with may on the labour market.

The Government cannot be secure where the governed cannot be free.

The Government that will arrest a man for lying against it, will not arrest a man for exaggerating its achievements.

The height of a nation is the living standard of its people.

The impregnable fortress of tyranny is vulnerable to the spirit of freedom.

The institutions of government must serve the people or else they are simply buildings.

The King has immunity from all summons, except that of nature.

The King summons anyone, the Toilet summons the King.

The light at the end of a tunnel may be an approaching train.

The lingua franca of the world is body language.

The longer an indolent leader remains in power, the longer is the road to progress.

The man to help the king is a threat to the men around the king.

The missiles of all economic reforms always land in the kitchen of the poor.

The moral status of a nation is the content of her responsibility to its people.

The mouth that feeds from a stolen corn, cannot insult a thief.

The Nation should be run better if not for the common good at least for the common safety.

The natural identity of an ideal youth is exuberance, energy and rebellion.

The next superpower usually watches over the slow decay of the reigning one.

The only way to eat a hot food is to start from the side ways.

The patient earth takes our fury and our body.

The people are the black box of a defunct Government.

The people can't know when the economy is bad, where they have never known when its good.

The people can't know when the economy is bad, where they have never known when its good.

The poor battles with poverty, the rich battles with the poor.

The poor does not need the truth, they are the truth.

The power of freedom is in the power of its dominion.

The protester is the tallest of all men.

The quality of contents of a refuse dumb is the quality of life of the people in its location.

The resume of an applicant only contains his good side.

The Rich are the Citizens, the poor are the countrymen.

The seed of revolution sprout from the heap of rubbish of the system.

The stanching smell of spilled human blood cannot be deodorized by anything but justice.

The statue of liberty should be sighted in the moral conduct of a free nation.

The threatening storm of a democracy is the expedient subversion of its constitutional principles.

The Throne and the Toilet are of equal importance to the King.

The transparency of a government is in the morality of its characters.

The truth can set you free and can get you into trouble.

The truth is of the Lord, justice is of the Judge.

The truth of a nation is the state of its people.

The tyranny of fear sustains the tyranny of violence.

The virus of power is forgetting those who hitherto stood by you.

The will of the people supersedes the good of the people.

The world can never be free from its trouble, but you can be free from the world of trouble.

There are critical moments that its recommended to throw away the message and the messenger.

There are loyalists to the king and Loyalists to the Crown, it takes wisdom for the King to know.

There can't be National security without social security.

There is no freedom in poverty.

Thieving in government is a full time engagement.

Those who deserve your anger are those who deserve your votes.

Those who want constructive criticisms should not unleash destructive governance.

To perform an oversight function, you have to fly and no bird can fly with a bullion van.

To resist corruption, resist the pressure to appease the wants of family and friends.

To some people, being in Government is survival.

To suspend a protest without achieving its aim is to feed some oxygen to a dying demon.

To the needy, what you give is what matters and not what you have.

Under a thieving Government, the strong room of a nation has many windows.

Under capitalism you can only chose which of the corruption to fight.

Unleashed evil first devours the poor, then the Rich.

Until every word of a constitution is made by the people, it cannot be said to be of the people.

Voice of a hired crowd is not a voice of God.

We always need peace, harmony and togetherness, but not between the Government and opposition.

We are not designed to be the same, but to pursue common goals.

We cannot protect our individual beliefs, in the face of a common tragedy.

We fought to bring democracy and freedom to our country, it appears we now have to fight to save both the country and the democracy.

What the army is to a nation is what the protester is to democracy.

Whatever is happening here, had happened somewhere and will happen elsewhere.

When a good man is hired to defend a lie, he first auctions his morality.

When a Government borrows to build infrastructure, it leaves behind a Building in its credit and a debt to be paid.

When a Government can't find a solution, it finds a scapegoat.

When a Government clamp down on the media, it down grades it status in the eyes of the world.

When a Government couldn't deliver on any of its promises, it will claim to have laid a foundation.

When a Government fails, it should be condemned by the people. When a Government delivers, it should appreciate the people.

When a Government habours criminals, the nation becomes a gang land.

When a Government is run by Technocrats, people are seen as figures.

When a King is disconnected from his people, he depends on aides about the Sun.

When a Leader fails, nobody blames the advisers.

When a Leader is long disconnected from his people, he must seek protection against his people.

When a leader is protected from the hands of his people, he does not have the Hearts of his people.

When a leader serves many, a many will like him to stay. When a leader serves a few, a few will like him to stay.

When a menace edges towards the leaders, a solution is near.

When a parliament is made up of old people, the nation gets their sleepy experience.

When a political party is about a personality, everything there is taken personally.

When a preacher is on state pay roll, all sermons is about the past.

When a president rule for long, the Government get wrinkles.

When a protester is shot, a heart is shut.

When a public officer refused to resign from a corrupt Government until it crashes with him, he loses all claims to been different.

When a rich man issued a bounce cheque, the Bankers return it with smile. When a poor man does same, they quote the law.

When a saint work for the devil, the difference won't be clear.

When a snake approaches a crippler, you will know of ability in disability.

When a Tiger invites you for dinner, go with a spoon and a spear.

When a war becomes a business, human lives becomes the commodity.

When all a leader does is lay a foundation, he has done what many can.

When an Ivory Tower sales its ivory, it simply became a tower.

When crisis comes, some leaders look for solutions, some look for scapegoats.

When ethics is removed from Business, it becomes a crime.

When everyone is silenced, a whistle is courage.

When hoodlums hijack a peaceful protest, they do what the rulers do.

When justice is frozen, overheat the polity.

When leaders are without solution, the solution is without those leaders.

When Leaders become thieves, the Land needs reform. When thieves become leaders, the land needs revolt.

When leaders become thieves, the land needs reform; when thieves become leaders, the land needs revolt.

When leaders take a wrong step, the nation takes a wrong turn.

When moral authority is lost, moral force will emerge.

When people fail to plan for old age, you find them in politics.

When security agents are overwhelmed, they call their job a collective responsibility.

When some people go into Government with a Bag of honour, they empty it for a stash of cash.

When the government pull the rug off the peoples feet, the people should fall on the government.

When the King fouls the air, only the courageous blocks his nose.

When the king is out of the toilet, the most loyal is best trusted to flush.

When the king you know is no more, exchange your houses for cattle.

When the king you know is out of power, exchange your horses for cattle.

When the Media bestow laurels on politicians and tycoons, who is left to be scrutinized.

When the rich give to the subjects its generosity, when they give to the King its investment.

When there's too many caps to wear, many will not be worn.

When thieves run a state, everything is done in the guise.

When thieving leaders also demand respect, they are defecating on your sorrow.

When Third world leaders buy private jets, is to fly over the public problem.

When you fail to stand up to injustice, you must sit to absorb its outcome.

When you justify your cause with violence, you justify others causes with violence.

When you kill a Lion, go to sleep, when u injure a Lion, stay awake.

When women protest naked, they will attract the ears of the Government and the eyes of the people.

When you appoint your kinsmen into office, they will last before the kinsmen of others come.

When you are in power, your word is power, when out of power, your word is sour.

When you dine with the devil, you grow a horn.

When you enthrone a butcher in power, you should not disgust the sight of blood.

When you Gossip about the King, you have given a favour seeker a meal ticket.

When you have a corrupt president, you run to the parliament, when you have a corrupt parliament your run to God.

When you make a promise, your integrity is on the gallow, when u fulfill it, its rescued.

When you raise a placard on the street, the palace reads your notes.

When you raise expectation, you have run into a debt.

When you walk for freedom, you are walking out on tyranny.

When your leg steps on Banana peel, let your hands first touch the ground.

Where a Nation's wealth will not be spread by the Government, will be spread by a mob.

Where judges can be bought, justice can be sold.

Where only the rich can afford a lawyer, justice comes at a price.

Where politics is about making money, Governance is about making profit.

Where politics is about making money, Governance is about making profit.

Where rogues rules, pick pockets are counted as saints.

Where the leaders do everything to amass, the led will do everything to survive.

Where the people lament and the Government lament, there is no Government.

Where the poor breeds the poor, a dynasty of poverty is founded.

Where the private sector is sustained by public money, there is no private sector.

Where views are suppressed, Guns will be expressed.

Wherever there is gaping contrast between the rich and the poor, its one country two systems.

Whoever will give u a dinner, will provide you with spoon, Devils don't accept long spoon.

You can choose not to bother about how your country is governed, but you can't choose not to feel it.

You can dream, you can hope but you must work it.

You can have a leader without power and a power without a leader.

You are without a vote, you are without a voice.

You can't build a holy city on a stolen land.

You can't free a people by killing them.

You can't win a clean race with a stolen horse.

You cannot teach a famished man how to fish.

You can't enrich a nation by impoverishing it's people.

You can't free a people by killing them.

You do not scratch the back of a tiger and expect it to scratch you back.

You gag the media, you strangle democracy.

You must know your rights before you fight for it.

You question power, you challenge power then you can dilute the acid of power.

You sell your vote, you lose your right to question your government.

People

A barman knows those a preacher doesn't.

A basket baller needs the qualities of a carmel, a fox and a bird.

A black pen can't write on a black paper. A white pen can't write on a white paper.

A Coconut is a man with hard outer soft inner.

A coward is a man born with a defect.

A democratic state binds its future to the aspirations of its people and not the ambition of its leader.

A dignitary lying in state is a dignitary who can't be helped by the state.

A dream that is not for the good of others is simply an ambition.

A Driver can never be sleepy on a rough road.

A friend of a policeman is not safer than his enemy.

A generation that will have a debt to pay, will have no respect to pay.

A Government not about the people cannot be said to be the nation.

A half dressed woman has a balance of half honour.

A hand used to charity will not be used to work.

A judge and an editor can only work at what is presented.

A known enemy is a visible danger.

A man chased by a Lion only look back to compare speed.

A man hired to speak for an unpopular king, have little time to Brush his mouth.

A man in power is the star of his moment.

A man is noticed by his claim and known by his conduct.

A man of history does not die at an instant.

A man on bail is an ATM machine.

A man out of power loves visitors.

A man who failed in life is hardly recognized by his ex-teacher.

A man who keep money in his cap, should avoid been chased.

A mango is a man with soft outer, hard inner.

A paw-paw is a man with soft outer, soft inner.

A people not armed with love, cannot defeat the demon of hatred.

A people not united by principles, will be divided by price.

A poor man has no enemy but his poverty.

A poor married woman earns more respect than a rich single woman.

A pretty woman is like a fragrance that attracts Bees.

A rich man that is faithful is a rare saint.

A slave master can sell the body but not the mind of the salve.

A slave ship can only carry the immorality of the slave master.

A snake charmer has no roommate but a snake charmer.

A stingy man is insulted only once, a generous man each time he pauses.

A surgeon has to painfully tear the body to reach to the ailment.

A Teacher's reward is in hand outs.

A thief, who donates to religious causes, is treated differently by the clerics.

A Tiger in prison becomes a cat.

A trader with a charitable heart may end up on charity.

A village cock crows at the sight of a lighted bulb.

A violinist teaches us to bend and get result.

A white man lives by monthly wages, an African lives by annual harvest.

A white man's family is his wife and children, an African family are all his kinsmen.

A wise man who sells Ice cream changes to umbrella when the rain starts falling.

A woman doesn't need to prove she's a woman, its a man that need to prove he is a man.

A woman half dressed attracts attention. A woman fully dressed attracts curiosity.

A woman politician and an actress share a lot in common.

A woman's stretch marks is a notification stamp.

After family feast, a white husband can pack plates and wash dishes, in Africa its the wife's duty.

All rockets need pressure to ascend.

An accomplished man with ambition is still on a journey.

An angry man, an evil mind, a loaded Gun, an infamy.

An evil mind will sometimes beat the best of technology.

An independent woman is a man.

An old man always thinks young girls are rude.

An old man in a sport car is money coming late.

An old man talks much and sleeps much on Bed.

An oppressed people are like a shaken bottle of wine.

An Ugly Rich Man is Handsomely attractive.

At the twilight of a man's life, he will sense the fact that he doesn't belong anymore.

Attention and swiftness is the survival secret of a matador.

Body builders don't believe all men are equal.

By sitting down to play, a pianist defies the problem of the world.

Children are happier if they inherited no wealth and no debt.

Children of the whites are not to be beaten, An African child must shape up by all means.

Count your life by your count in other lives.

Crowning a lunatic does not make him sane.

Death has a habit of first consuming those you closely know.

Die with a wealth of honor.

Disappointment only comes from people you believe in.

Doctors and Bankers know what is in the belly of a Big man.

Don't wait for death to celebrate your hero.

Every individual is naturally endowed with unique qualities of greatness that he or she only need to explore.

Every man must find a space for his life or create one for himself.

Few campus stars become life stars.

Foes choose invasion, loyalists choose palace coups.

For a white man, greeting is courtesy, for an African, its morality.

For all you are somewhere, you remain unknown to someone elsewhere.

For every celebrated hero, there are many more that will never be known.

Friends shape our compassion, foes shape our vigilance.

From the best of men to the worst, there's lesson to learn in every life.

God want by your heart and justice need your voice.

Good friends are umbrellas.

Gossip and rumour need no phone service providers to spread.

Hard times tests our weakness.

Have no fear of the enemy because the enemy has fear of your confidence.

He talks when he should be silent, is a fool, he is silent when he should talk, is a coward

He who kills and run away live to be killed another day.

History remembers good people and evil people and not normal people.

Human mind responds to human passion.

If a Bald is not about genes, about wealth or about intelligence, it is about vitamins deficiency.

If a man has no conscience, then he is simply a con.

If there exist a perfect man, he will claim to be a god.

If you are trusted, you are entrusted.

If you believe in protest, you don't have to wait to be led.

If you come with a truck of food and camera to Africa, you become a world humanitarian.

If you die free of debt, you die rich.

If you have faith and fear, you have more fear than faith.

If you hold a minority view, you are either right or mad.

If you keep on dancing to the drum beat with your eyes closed, you will end up in a pit.

If you want a serious message to seriously reach to all women, draft fashion designers.

If your relation heads your business, you may have to choose between relationship or business.

If your star is not to succeed now and fail later, then your star is to fail now and succeed later.

Ignorance resides in the man who thinks he knows all.

In a woman's handbag, there is everything except a first aid kit.

In a world of make up, ugly people are becoming extinct.

In conscience and courage, men light up the dark spots of their nation.

In dreams and in Chinese movies, people can fly.

In life, some roads lead to a new beginning, some to a circle, some to a terminal.

In Life, there are people you are better off not knowing.

In places where people do not matter, it's things that matter.

In the female section of the prison yard, women inmates are not allowed to bring in bananas.

In the turbulence of life, your dreams find its fate.

In the village, whatever you do is kept for your great grand children to know.

In the white world, a man and a woman marry, in the African world, its two families that marry.

In the white world, Gays and Animals have rights, in the African world, Gays and animals have no rights.

In the white world, old people die in old peoples' home, in the African world, old people die in family home.

In the white world, the husband and wife are equal, in d African world, the husband is the undisputed Head of the family.

In the white world, woman marries a man, in African world, man marries a woman.

It takes a longer time to discover the good qualities of an ugly woman.

It's not easy for the poor to be honest and its difficult to find a honest rich man.

It's useless for a man to know the job only when he lost the job.

Leadership is a rare opportunity, to reveal your genius and unveil that of others.

Life is not lived by years but by moment of every breath, every heart beat.

Living in prison is like been in a lift, you breath with unknown people in an enclosure.

Man cannot live by bread alone, he will need a cup of tea.

Men don't like to be caught staying long before a mirror.

Men don't run away from a Naked mad woman. Women run away from a naked madman.

Men of God are not necessarily God fearing Men.

Men with a conviction of truth cannot be sentenced to silence.

Microscope for microbes, mind for matters.

Most times God comes in form of resolve of a people.

Most women don't use the radio, they get their news briefing from the saloon.

No black man anywhere can grow beyond the plight of his race in Africa.

No man of money leaves a will to be buried with money.

No man or woman can be on the last page of the Economist alive.

No matter what's it's done, a lying mouth can't be brushed.

No one believe the world is ending soon like a bankrupt man.

No one wishes you long life like the man who gave you a loan.

Nobody remembers the Birthday of a Man out of power, but his family.

Of all the things that interest most women in newspapers are gossips and fashion.

Old men have no future.

Our African heritage demands faithfulness from a wife and responsibility from a husband.

Our individual achievements dissolve in the collective waste of our generation.

Our religion does not reveals who we are but what we should be.

Overcoming temptation is a resistance movement.

People in the city have enough time for plots and those in the village have enough time for gossip.

Our parents inspire us, our children tame us.

People who don't dance in the public, dance when they are alone.

People who forgive are unpredictable, people who avenge are predictable.

People with longer Throats, gets more hooked by a longer borne.

Posterity shapes the thoughts of the white man, Ancestors shape the thoughts of an African.

Poverty and affluence have an equal capacity to influence the mind of Man.

Praise singers get the most in religion and in politics.

Scrutiny is at the door step of he who lay claim to purity.

Some people have to die for the world to love them.

Sometimes we are far away from the people we know and close to the people we don't.

Reality is scary to a man of beer.

Rewarding some people entails appointing them to lucrative offices to help themselves and help the president men.

Share your sorrow with your friends and your joy with everyone.

Social networking is edging the world to a chaotic order.

Some are born great, some achieve greatness, some throw great nation to the path of perdition.

Some fools understand Silence and some don't.

Some leaders epitaph is engraved in the hearts of their people.

Some people are more appealing by shutting their mouth.

Some people are more appealing keeping quiet.

Some people are so short of morals that you have to bend before they understand you.

Some poverty is about needs, some about want.

Some will be remembered for what they did, some for what they refused to do.

Somebody oppresses you, somebody fights for you shows how submissive and dependent you are.

Speak the truth to your foes and make it a rule to your friends.

Standing in the Middle of the road is the art of a Donkey.

Starve the lazy to awaken his spirit.

Suicide is of the weak without the courage to live.

Sycophants are not pricked by conscience.

Technology improves many lives and destroyed many livelihoods.

The ants teach us about the strength in team spirit.

The belief that you can overcome, makes you an overcomer.

The chains of the slave is the gold of his innocence.

The dead are remembered for what they live or die for.

The death of a Lion is confirmed with a stone, not a stick.

The evil of man makes mortality the only means of continuity.

The faith of a man is his version of the truth.

The family accelerates and decelerates a Man.

The first principle of a rich man is preservation and of a poor man aspiration.

The God of the rich is the same God of the poor.

The Heart beat faster when an old man tries to be a young man.

The man who does not know you will appreciate your generosity more than the man who knows you.

The mirror of a starving child in Africa, is the image of all black billionaires.

The people are the black box of a defunct Government.

The plantation of the slave master is his crime scene.

The poor can't walk high like the rich, the rich can't walk low like the poor.

The power of evil is in the fear of its victims.

The problem of those who have choices is choice, the problem of those with choice is choices.

The protester is the Guardian of democracy.

The rich also cry, mostly of joy.

The rot in wealth is glossed in hardwork.

The signs of Men only or Women only is discrimination.

The static life under the bridge threaten the moving life above the bridge.

The static life under the tree, there is no shade for the rich.

The strength of a woman is in her weakness, the weakness of a man is in his strength.

The time is up when people are fed up.

The truth that works is the one you tell yourself.

The two fingers that can snap, have been approved from creation.

The way you drive reflects your attitude to life.

The white man lives by needs, the African lives by excess.

The white man restrict the number of his children to his plan, An African crowd them to the care of the Heaven.

The white man's believes in proofs, the African believes in beliefs.

The will of the people supersedes the good of the people.

The words of a jilted woman can roast a fish.

The world is changed by those who dare.

The world of a tribesman is the wall of his tribe.

The young, know small and wish much. The old know much and wish small.

There are gentlemen but no gentle ladies because all ladies are assumed to be gentle.

There are gentlemen but no gentle ladies because all ladies are assumed to be gentle.

There are times peace becomes a form of cowardice but no time has a war becomes the only means of bravery.

There's no better time to gauge the moral claim of a man, than when it's time to tell the truth to his kinsman in power.

They have not dread the day, the haves dread the night.

Things we treasure are the burdens of our soul.

Those who are paid to work for the devil, will spend the proceed in evil services.

Those who count on you count on your integrity.

Those who deserve help are those need it temporarily.

Those who score goals keep in mind the opposition of the goal keeper.

Those who toil appreciates generosity better.

Three steps to success; ideas, dreams, resilience.

Time overcomes man, faith overcomes time.

To a thirsty man, water is thicker than blood.

To aim higher, you must pull the catapult string harder.

To earn money is to earn money, to earn respect is to earn people.

To earn money is to earn money, to earn respect is to earn people.

To know little is not to know nothing. To know much is not to know all.

To reach to a height higher than your own, you have to stretch yourself further.

To resolve to change your life for the better is to resolve to grow.

To survive, adapt to change, to excel, lead the change.

To tell the truth and run is conscience, to tell the truth and stand is courage

To the man you are not feeding, you cannot be the richest man in the world.

Truth can bring people together, truth can tear people apart.

Truth can bring people together, truth can tear people apart.

Walk through the thick forest of your troubles with determination that where the solution lays.

Warriors fall, Empires crumble under the seductive force of a woman.

We are many things when alive, we are one thing when dead.

When a man is out of power, he searches for relevance and friends.

When a man is out of power, take his advice and take back his criticism.

When a man made up his mind to accept a Government appointment, he calls it a national service.

When a mother dies, the train that brought you had departed to eternity.

When a people prefers sports to politics, the spirit of governance is gone.

When a policeman is caught between duty and friendship, he sends his colleague to do the job and turn the other side.

When an innocent man is jailed, a nation's conscience is stained.

When Devine words meet human interpretation, the end result can be anything.

When false prophesy comes to falsehood, the false prophet attribute it to prayers.

When in the mosque or church, we are saintly, when out of it, we become humanly.

When it's your time on the stage of life, the world cast it's light on you.

When most people pass by a prison, they think it belongs to others.

When people cannot unlock your secret, they invent a key to it.

When some people speak, they want your attention. When some people speak, they want attention.

When some people talk, they want to be listened. When some people talk, they want to be heard.

When the Gap between the rich and the poor keeps widening, so will be their peace.

When the king u know is out of power, exchange your horses for cattles.

When the poor sleep under the tree, there no shade left for the rich.

When visiting a white man house, you must seek appointment, in Africa appointment is not needed.

When you appoint a man into office because of loyalty, that may be the only thing he has.

When you are without a conscience, you are without a shame.

When you are finding a reason to attach to your deed, your deed have no justification.

When you breast the tape and win the trophy in life, the next challenge is to keep it.

When you bury a king, you then know he was never a King.

When you can't criticize your own, you lose the moral right to criticize that of others.

When you default on a Loan, opt to see the devil than hear the knock of your banker.

When you eat out with a white man, ensure you have money to settle your bill, in Africa d bill for a group feast is footed by one.

When you give nonstop, you become bankrupt, when u take nonstop u become a beggar.

When you have an hour to speak about what u know, don't just fill up the time with what you don't know.

When you hit the age of forty, you have arrived the future.

When you mistakenly match on the tail of a snake, you should deliberately go for the head.

When you run out of ideas, you run out of progress

When you shield a man from all problems of life, you have created for him a problem of dependency.

When you stop to help a pregnant mad woman, some people will insinuate something.

Where people faces each other, without talking to each other is in the train.

Where rogues rules, pick pockets are counted as saints.

Where you stand today determines where you sit tomorrow.

White world, noise is pollution, African world, noise is life.

Who does not appreciate little, will not appreciate much.

With social justice, a loaf can feed many, without it, bakery can feed none.

You can be living in the open but sunk in a deep pit.

You can fail to win but don't fail to pick up.

You can hide a secret in the internet because nobody will believe it if is there.

You can know a person without understanding him. You can understand a person without knowing him.

You can live with a thief for a day, you cannot live with a hypocrite for a moment.

You can motivate a failed man, not a dead man.

You can neither predict God nor the mind of a Human being.

You can't get the attention of a man with an eviction notice in a sermon.

You can't score goals without aiming and shooting at the post.

You cannot stand on the Beach if something is not holding back the waters.

You can't be fed and be respected.

You can't excel if all you do is what all are doing.

You can't fly with wet wings.

You can't get all you want in Life but all you get is all you need.

You divorce a white woman, she goes with part of the family wealth, you divorce an African woman, she finds her way.

You don't need a religion to do good, but you need a religion to avoid evil.

You must be interested in the character of your leader like the senility of your pilot.

Your extra ordinary day is someone's ordinary day.

Your father likes women is a pride. your mother likes men is a shame.

Peace

A decaying garbage breeds worms, a decaying society breeds Gunmen.

A force can command the body, not the spirit.

A Gun can silence a voice, a voice can silence a Gun.

A gun man can do the damage of an army.

A hand can pull the trigger, a hand can push for peace.

A Hand on the trigger, a life on the line.

A hand stained with blood cannot open the door of heaven.

A lone man, with a Gun and a mindset is a Canon.

A nation in search of peace is a nation in need of justice.

A people divided, a people retarded.

A prevailing injustice is a pending war.

One angry man in a nation is a potential for a woe.

A torrent of voice for peace can extinguish the ragging flames of terror.

All bloodshed must stop, except that of women.

All religion advocates peace and all men of war belong to a religion.

All religions lay claim to peace in perpetually violent world.

Among those who daily ask for the Lord's forgiveness, are those who won't forgive.

Any occurrence of violence, upgrades the status of beasts and downgrades the status of Man in the animal kingdom.

Arms trade comes before war, arms trade comes after war.

Because of one, the Lord can forgive many. because of one, Man can kill many.

Bridge of moderation is broken by those who know too much and those who know too little.

Bullets kill the subjects, words kill the king.

Death of the innocent is a sword in the heart of a nation.

Entrench justice in the Land and the Roses of peace will flourish unattended.

Events like these, a day like this, a prayer for peace.

Every drop of blood of the innocent stains the conscience of our leaders.

Every life lost to murder questions the protective responsibility of the state.

For every life wasted by man, the gap to the beast is narrowed.

For peace, counsel the blasphemed on forgiveness and the blasphemer on consequences.

Free society embraces the beauty of diversity, not the evil of divisiveness.

Great empires were one time defeated.

He who kills and runaway, lives to be killed another day.

If your religion actually gives you peace, share that peace with others.

In Beirut and in Belfast, faith is a sword.

In revenge, you are equal to your foe. In forgiveness, you are above him.

In some huts you have more peace than in some mansions.

In the Land of Guns, every head is on the cross hair.

In times of peace, people die in queues, in times of war, in droves.

Insurgency undermines expression, expression undermine insurgency.

It's the Heart that chooses to forgive and the Brain that chooses to forget.

Let your beliefs take you to your beliefs and give others their peace.

Maiduguri, a city where soldiers protect police stations.

Men of peace are the saviours of a violent world.

Murder is ladder to the Lucifer, not Lord.

No ideal can float on the blood of the innocent.

No Nation will go to war if it seeks the opinion of a soldier's mother.

Our religion does not reveals who we are but what we should be.

Our society needs to reach a menopause, so that all blooshed must end.

Our spiritual significance makes no meaning without our moral significance.

Our woes our history, our peace our wisdom.

Peace Between the rich and the poor is an interval of cease fire.

Peace is a treasure most appreciated in its absence.

Peace is nothing other than something on which everything depends upon.

Peace is peace. War is war. War and peace is love.

People who forgive are unpredictable, people who avenge are predictable.

Physical force kills, moral force wins.

Scriptures and money are seriously competing for the Hearts of men.

Silence in the midst of evil is conscience on the retreat.

Some people touch the lives of others, some torches them.

Some wars are civil not because they are civil.

The best décor interior needs is peace.

The Boat of fear, the mast of silence, keeps afloat the cargo of violence.

The bulb of peace lightens the darkest of houses.

The chain of peace is making peace with our neighbors.

The conscience of those who kill and run, acknowledges the existence of repercussion.

The greatest feat humanity can achieve, is to record a single day, in our billion year history, when no one kills.

The power of evil is in the fear of its victims.

The stanching smell of spilled human blood cannot be deodorized by anything but justice.

The strength of an army is the morality of its force and its conduct.

The Terrorist wins over a nation that has to suspend its cherished values to fight him.

The vase can only last in a peaceful home, not just a beautiful one.

The very fact that I can commit sin and ask for forgiveness from God, morally affects my passion for revenge.

The world is an old fabric, when one part is sown, another part is torn.

The world is unsafe from those who know too much and too little about God.

There are moments a victory is not peace.

There are times peace becomes a form of cowardice but no time has a war becomes the only means of bravery.

To bring down violence, you must stand up to it.

To disarm a madman, go with a Loaf of Bread and a sword.

To the war weary, peace is God.

To those born after a war, war is a tale.

War and peace is the ways of the world, till the end of the way and the world.

War is a wave, peace is a shore line.

War sits at the door step of a nation awashed with weapons.

We are Muslims, Christians, Jews, Buddists, Hindus but mankind actually live in the world of Cain and Abel.

We cannot protect our individual beliefs, in the face of a common tragedy.

We hold true to our beliefs in the hope that our belief is the truth.

Whatever a hostage does is of the gun not of the mind.

When a man shoots a Beehive, not even the innocents are safe.

When a slap remove your teeth, you can't turn the other cheek.

When a war is far away, many think of it as a chess.

When making peace between feuding thugs, ensure the spectators know your identity and mission.

When the innocent is killed, the flood gate of deaths is opened.

When you kill an innocent man, his spirit becomes your shadow.

When you live violence, you live with sorrow.

When you match for peace, you are matching on violence.

When your sense of justice is not universal, your sense of reasoning is narrow.

Where every house has a Gun, every house becomes a state.

Where guns are cheap, lives are cheap.

Where men of God kills, God has no men.

Where weapons are cheap, human lives are cheap.

With a clear conscience, you can successfully fly thru a storm.

With Land mines, a war never ends.

You can enforce an order, but peace can only be promoted.

You don't need a religion to do good, but you need a religion to avoid evil.

You live in infamy, you live on the run.

You owe to yourself the defence of your right and that of others.

Relationships

A chaste woman has a pin code.

A chaste woman not fed by men will be fed by angels.

A dosage of love soothes and commits the soul.

A faithful woman need no money but deserve all money needed for needs.

A husband is a man you know, then you don't know and then you know better.

A Husband living in his wife's house, learns to control his anger.

A jealous man is a loaded Gun.

A people not armed with love, cannot defeat the demon of hatred.

A possessive lover is a prison warden.

A sweet voice does not mean a pretty face.

A woman doesn't need to prove she's a woman, it's a man that need to prove he is a man.

A woman has the capacity to bring an emperor to his knees.

A woman in love can defy the world, a man in love can risk his world.

A woman who doesn't play hard to get is an answering machine.

A woman's single revenge is more painful than a man's catalogue.

Among many friends are truly few friends.

Ancient women test their men by their vigor, modern women test their men by maintenance cost.

Be not all wise in love, some level of idiocy spices it up.

Beauty contest reveals the best among those who compete.

Bedroom secrets are revealed on the maternity Bed.

Before scoring the Radio presenter with a sweet voice, see her physically

Behind every successful man, there's a nagging woman.

Being good to Girls comes with motives.

Cardiologists do not treat broken hearts.

Don't blame a woman for been in a hurry, beauty only last for a while

Don't blame women for hard to get, it's a filtration process.

Don't give your heart to a butcher.

Ego destroys marriages of rich couples.

Females like been stared at for long, except a female tiger.

Friends you can count on, are those that count.

Genuine Love needs no supervision or inspection.

Handsome men are presentable, Rich men, dependable and caring men, available.

If there is no ventilation in a relationship, there will be suffocation.

If you are tired of life, you are not in love.

If you marry early, you will miss adventure and gain Time.

If you marry late, you will give birth to your grand children.

In love, men give their passion, women give their heart.

In marriage justice do not necessarily leads to peace.

In Marriage, you willingly agree to loose your freedom and hope for happiness.

In modern day love, lovers need protection from each other.

In most times, women and buildings outlive men.

In relationships, failed expectations leads to secession.

Lesser communication is the first symptom of a dying love.

Love cages the beast in us, hate cages the humanity in us.

Love ends where the love stops.

Love frees the Heart from pain but commit it to a bond.

Love has a dual capability of making you sleep and sleepless.

Love is a full time job for a woman.

Love is a plane that can take you to the clouds.

Love is a universal accent.

Love is blind but Bills need sight.

Love is the only deepest pit you fall in order to meet a partner.

Lovers and mad people only see themselves in a crowd.

Lovers like astronauts, they go the moon.

Many Gentlemen are lost in the Game of hard to get.

Men are attracted by beauty and women by ability.

Men are too busy to visit the grave of their women and women are too scared to do so also.

Men conquer women, women win over the conqueror.

Men have more litres of sweat to shed, and women, tears.

Men love with their brain and women love with their hearts.

Men tell lies to get a woman, women tell lies to keep a man.

Men think a Woman's 'no' is yes or try again.

Men thinks women don't know, women thinks men know little.

Men with money have no time, men with time have no money.

Money can buy a love that is for sale.

Money is the root of all evil and equally so are Bills.

Monogamy is dictatorship, polygamy is crisis management.

Most women who turned down multitude of suitors, end up with the wrong one.

No true love if it's not like the teens love.

On matters of jealousy, women injure and men kill.

On wedding, you invite others, On divorce, others hear.

Once a Man beat a woman to right a wrong, it becomes the only way to right a wrong.

Only in love you can trust and still suspect.

Patient women always win, because they are in short supply.

Playboys are more tolerant to the game of hard to get than gentlemen.

Self harmsterms from self indulgence.

She who collects gifts, feels a commitment to pay it back.

The charming smile of a woman can demolish the rigid muzzles of a man.

The charming smile of a woman can demolish the rigid muzzles of a man.

The charming smile of a woman can demolish the rigid muzzles of a man.

The cost of marriage is not counted in marital life.

The Gold you bought for a woman yesterday will not save you from the Bronze you didn't buy today.

The Habits hiding in courtship are the Habits that explode marriages.

The integrity of a woman is with the honour of her man.

The pain of love is the relief of the soul.

The troubles of good relationship is the joy of togetherness.

There is a beast in every man and a demon in every woman.

There is never a shortage of men to marry, there's always a shortage of men needed for marriage.

There was world war one, world war two and lovers war that will never end.

Things we lose are things not meant to stay.

Those who play hard to get are won over by stubborn people.

To free body from a bad relationship, you have to first free your soul from it.

To the mother in-law, a wife is a beneficiary.

Toasting a woman in veil is a gamble.

We shed tears on same pillow that help us sleep.

What love have brought together, Bills must not put asunder.

When a husband rises from poverty to richness, the wife become the first beneficiary and the first casualty.

When a husband starts calling his wife a mummy, he means she is now a mama.

When a man cannot provide for his woman, the authority of his government is limited.

When a man cannot provide for his woman, the authority of his government is limited.

When a marriage is only about the children, the house becomes a day care.

When a pretty woman pass by a couple, peace is negative remark.

When a wife and a sister in-law quarrels, the mother in-law is interested in the verdict of the judge.

When a woman withstand the indescrition of a man, she become his sister or his foe.

When a women loses a Husband, the next to lose are his friends.

When an actress marries an actor, the marriage becomes a scene.

When in love, a man is on the grip, When in love a woman is under control.

When love enters the heart, it brings succour, when it exits, it leaves injury.

When Mr. wrong come at the right time, Mr Right will come at the wrong time.

When some realities set in, Love takes a flight.

When the wife is the bread winner, the husband lose many of his rights.

When we made up our mind that a man is good, we forget that he is human.

When you bring a flower to an African woman, you have to explain what it means.

When you choose to love a woman because she is clean, the love is conditional.

When you drink from the cup of love, it goes to the heart not the tummy.

When you fall in love, you are a martyr of your passion.

When you get a knock on the door of your heart, pip to see the stranger before you open.

When you have someone to love, you have a human intoxicant.

When you marry a girl because she is from a poor home, she will still be a typical woman.

When you marry a girl because she is from a rich home, you will have money and arrogance.

Whenever Love can't settle bills then Bills will settle lovers.

With humility, a woman can control a man.

Woman struggles to keep the love, man struggles to keep the woman.

Women acknowledge the problem of women by keeping few friends.

Women are not ingrates, they appreciate consistency in generosity.

Women below twenty four don't move around with a mirror, they are the mirrors.

Women can tell their friends how their husband snore, but men can't.

Women easily forgive the bad done to them and forget the good done to them.

Women fight their age with cream, Men fight theirs with herbs.

Women habitually request older men to prove their gender.

Women know women better, that is why most women have few women friends.

Women think of men as unreliable, men think of women as ungrateful.

Women want fat account but flat tummy.

Women watch their weight to be watched.

You can't all have your way, that's why pretty women also visit the toilet.

You can't close your eyes if the mouth you are kissing is not clean.

You can't hurry a woman to a journey, she will take her time to waste your time.

You won't know a woman has good memory until a day of quarrel.

Your enemy is your friend, your friend is your enemy; that's husband and wife.

Your secrets are your mysteries.

Life

A Big car parked may have no fuel.

A Bird prefers the Hardship of freedom than the luxury of a cage.

A bony fish can't be eaten in a hurry.

A book is not a cap to just fit in to your head, you must sit down for it.

A clean heart is the best guarantee against treachery.

A coconut fears no fall.

A dead man is at least free from the fear of dying.

A dead man lives in those hearts he made a presence.

A dead man speaks by his trail.

A dog registers a car with a pee on the tyre.

A dripping tap can flood the whole house.

A farmer feeds the body, a preacher feeds the soul.

A fart cannot blow a balloon.

A favour seeker cannot tell the king the truth.

A grey hair is a spice.

A gun is simply a metal, until used.

A gushing river gets calm upon meeting a sea.

A head used to burden doesn't appreciate a cap.

A heart that beats is never lonely.

A heartache can lead to a headache. A headache can lead to a heartache.

A helping hand is from a humble heart.

A hospital bed is a gateway.

A leader who can't die for you, does not live for you.

A life of money is a life of price.

A life on the screen is a life on the scream.

A Life time can't pay back the service of a mother.

A life time cannot pay a mother.

A life without a plan is a life on others plan.

A little control the soul, a much indulges it.

A loving wife is the best of all cooks.

A man asleep is at the mercy of those awake.

A Man's face tells nothing about his heart.

A marabout will always say you have enemies.

A moment can change a history of a hundred of years.

A new driver should learn on rough road first.

A New year in Life is turning a new Life.

A new year is a closed package that will be unfolded in each of its day.

A new year is simply a new day like any other day.

A prevailing evil is a call to conscience.

A saint who does not want to be seen as a sinner want to be seen as a god.

A scream in the Toilet is not a call for help.

A shepherd guides and guards.

A sick body affects the man, a sick soul affects humanity.

A soap alone does not clean the body.

A soap does not clean the soul.

A speech that adds no value to the Life of its audience is a belch.

A star who touches the lives of others is the superstar.

A tenant is a normad.

A tenant who fries eggs in a poor neighborhood should learn to keep the aroma within her room.

A Toilet is a delivery room as well as an emergency ward.

A train does not stop for a car.

A village nurse is a doctor.

A widows might is the mightiest of all the might of giving.

A woman carrying a basket of eggs, should ignore the insult from woman carrying a basket of stones.

A woman's kitchen is her shrine.

A woman's stretch marks is a notification stamp.

A word in our heart is your slave. A word out of your mouth is your master.

A word is an arrow.

Actresses marriages does not last because their life is in stages.

After the flavor, a candy is a jaw exercise.

All Holy Lands only welcome people who intend going back to their homes after pilgrimage.

Amending a stolen goods does not make it your own.

Among nations and within people, there is no massive wealth without some level of criminality.

An account in debit is a paradise lost.

An elder sister who is unmarried will discourage a younger sister who wants to marry.

An empty house cannot stand for long.

An old man either depend on his youthful investment, his children or on charity.

An old man either depend on his youthful investment, his children or on charity.

An orphan have a world for a parent.

As long as you are alive, you are close no matter how far you live.

As the sun sets in one village, it is rising in another.

As you can change your furniture, you can change your life.

At the end of a tunnel, you either get light or another tunnel.

At the twilight of our lives, we battle stay alive.

Bad habit is infectious.

Bad habit is radioactive.

Be inspired and be yourself.

Been good to a leper excludes a handshake.

Benevolence does not necessarily establishes morality.

Betrayal succeeds because the borderline with friends is naturally unguarded.

Blocks of stolen wealth can't build a hut of integrity.

Borrow money from a woman in a room, you will hear it in the Market.

Both the wife of a poor man and the rich man have to battle with flies invading their homes.

By the little good you do to those you met, you spray goodness to the greater world.

By the little good you do to those you met, you spray goodness to the greater world.

By the meeting with different kind of people along our journey of life, we advance our knowledge of life.

Cemetery is like a parking lot, but a permanent one.

Comedians cage your realities just for a moment.

Coming down the stair case needs lesser effort.

Conscience is the best admonisher.

Death is an everyday stranger.

Death, a mystery no man unravels yet.

Descending from the slope needs no much effort.

Desire is the most popular of gods.

Determination is the battery of Life.

Don't hurry towards an injured prey, it may have escaped from a bigger prey.

Each man live his time and leave.

Eat grass and sleep if that is more dignifying.

Eba doesn't need the protocol of kola nut.

Enjoy living in the shadows for a while before the Sun moves.

Even in the market of stolen goods, customer is the king.

Every family is a fragment of another.

Every family must ultimately dissolve to form another family.

Every individual is naturally endowed with unique qualities of greatness that he or she only need to explore.

Every man must find a space for his life or create one for himself.

Every morning you wake up to the uncertainties and challenges of your existence.

Every new day comes with its package of event.

Every new year comes with a new lists of those it will build and those it will destroy.

Everyman is built in with the capacity to change his life, on pressing the button of his resolve.

Everyman is built in with the capacity to change his life, on pressing the button of his resolve.

Everyone is once given an opportunity in life to use it or to waste it.

Evicting notice evicts all our problems except one.

Expect your foes to celebrate your death and hope that your friends remember your family.

Expectation and hope is for the living mind.

Faith is of the mind for the body.

Fate has no insurance.

Fathers' day to others, day of infamy to us.

Few must die for many to live or many will die for few to live.

Find my body in my grave, find my soul in my calling.

Follow your heart but with your brain.

For all your troubles in life is but a wish for someone.

For every burglar inside the house, there is another one outside the door.

For those who died in plane crash, we pray for them. For their families we show them love and encourage them to move on.

For treasures of the dessert, go with a Carmel, not a chariot.

For whatever you feel attach to, your life will depend on it.

For your journey to the future, take along with you lessons of your past.

Forget your tragedies when in motion but remember them when you pause.

From the same tree, leaves fall at different times and intervals.

Genuine Compassion to one needy person is compassion to the whole of humanity.

Get it, use it, loose it and account for it, that is vanity.

Give a good advice even if it is ignored, you have registered you innocence.

Give your child a loaf of bread and take him to see a wheat field and a Bakery.

Given out things you don't like, is a relief, Given out things you like, is a sacrifice.

God is of the soul and religion is of the body.

Good friends are umbrellas.

Good is planned, evil is plotted.

Gory scenes pulls crowds and disgust.

Grow, glow, dim and fade away, that's life.

Happiness is not a continues thing, it comes at an interval of other things.

Happiness is not a continues thing, it comes at an interval of other things.

Happiness is not about money but money can bring happiness.

Happiness is not about money but money can bring happiness.

Hardships are meant to generate ideas of invention or of revolt.

He that gives Life should be He that takes Life.

He who does not have a mind of his own, does not have a Heart of his own.

Heaven is a consolation for the poor.

Hope is a dimple of the soul, despair is its wrinkle.

Human intelligence is by itself a divine gift.

Hurry to your dream but be patient with result.

Ideas only come from imaginative minds.

If a cake is bad, you can eat it and have it back.

If a cake is bad, you can eat it and have it back.

If all your life is about yourself, you should be ready to bury yourself when dead.

If all your life is about yourself, you should be ready to bury yourself when dead.

If life is a movie, no hero will die.

If only the dead can talk, the world will be better or worse

If the Lord wanted the tongue to be without restrain, He couldn't have hinged it in the mouth.

If you are dancing the music that only you can hear, people will rate you a madman.

If you are lacking in courage to stand up for good, you should not be found in the service of evil.

If you are really climbing up a mountain so high, just look ahead.

If you are without a mother, you are without a shoulder to cry to.

If you are without a mother, you are without a shoulder to cry to.

If you are without foes, you are without worth.

If you believe in the strength of your beliefs, it should co exist with other beliefs.

If you believe that only when you sell yourself can you buy your food, so shall it be.

If you bury the truth under the rock, it will sip in form of water.

If you can have a rat in your room, you can have a snake in your room.

If you can have a rat in your room, you can have a snake in your room.

If you constantly remind yourself that life is a transit, you'll free yourself of its stress.

If you don't depend on one God, you will depend on many gods.

If you have faith and fear, you have more fear than faith.

If you have hope, you have reserved a seat in the future.

If you have never been in jail, you have never been in trouble.

If you like to pick pockets, you will someday meet a blade.

If you live life to its purpose, there's nothing to miss of it.

If you must win at all cost, you will lose at no cost.

If you want to loose weight fast, get into trouble.

If you wasted thirty nine years of your life, life begins at forty.

If your hand is longer than your pocket you get a hole.

If your life is ruled by money, you are a commodity.

If your star is not to succeed now and fail later, then your star is to fail now and succeed later.

In a fast moving world, most things passes before they are understood.

In a greedy society, a patient Dog die hungrily.

In a village full of beauty, you look for substance.

In greed and obsessions, the spirit wanes.

In judging people, you don't use the ways of the Courts.

In life, your senses are your traffic warden.

In prayer or in Beer, men seeks solace from the troubles of life.

In prison, there is no New day, except the freedom day.

In religion, you are demanded to believe what you didn't see.

In speed, your life is on your tyres, in slow, it's on your breaks.

In terms of faith, all your eggs must be in one basket.

In the battle to succeed in Life, there will always be opposing bullets in advance.

In the Bosom of the Earth shall our body finds its rest and in the Lord, our soul.

In the market, a woman has enough time to spend, not to be cheated.

In the prison, you Learn the art of sharing a cup with people who hate to brush.

In the pubs, there are permanent friends and permanent interest.

In the village, whatever you do is kept in the file of your family.

In the waves of daily challenges, a life is lived.

In times of need, a little is worth a much.

In troubling times, history is fishing for a leader.

In vanity, a transit become a destination.

In what you left, is how you lived.

It's easier to learn the language than live the culture.

It's only in religion, not History that people shed tears for past events of thousand years.

It's still the soul that can heal a broken heart.

Its human to worry, but worrying won't end the worlds worries.

Its human to worry, but worrying won't end the worlds worries.

Kindness is an attitude.

Learning to live without your indulgence is the first lesson of prison life.

Let your life preach your faith.

Life comes with checks, trees slowing the wind.

Life is a limited space to stamp your presence.

Life is a runway, do your cat walk and leave.

Life is a short but eventful trip.

Life is an ever moving matter, it goes on.

Life is nothing but a meant to lived for its purpose.

Life is refined by lessons learnt from experiences.

Life is the history of man; man is the history of a woman.

Live a little in need, live a large in spirit.

Live life to the fullest, there's enough time to rest when dead.

Living happily ever after is only possible in lullabies.

Living with a clean mind is the best insurance against mischief.

Loving your neighbor like yourself is only possible in scriptures not in real life.

Luck is the god of the Gambler.

Man build a house, the Lord has the eternal list of its occupants.

Man build a house, the Lord has the eternal list of its occupants.

Material acquisitions ties down the soul to ephemerals.

Money removes the problems of needs and brings the problems of abundance.

Money removes the problems of needs and brings the problems of abundance.

Money stolen is money to be wasted.

Morality is in no contention, it just stand out.

Mortality nullifies greed.

Most fatal sicknesses begins with signs we ignore.

Most of life is wasted in the pursuit of vanity and the preservation of it.

Most people eat up their mid age at youth age.

Mother gives love, father gives identity.

Nature destroys us to preserve us forever.

No coffin is designed with a safe.

No man lives beyond his time or dies ahead of his date.

No matter how high you fly in life, you are still close and heading to the ground.

Of all the human organs that forms the five senses, it's only the tongue. that is restricted and locked up in the mouth.

Of those things you do with energy, you will someday watch with crouch.

Old people are human archives.

Old photos are the best mirrors.

On a Horse with a Limited life span, we mount an unlimited burden of ambition.

Once status change, habit changes.

Once the Heart stops beating, everything stops singing.

Once used to easy money, never can you adjust to earned money.

Once you are baleful, all foods are tasteless.

Once you taken from the cult, you must give back to the cult.

One tree of truth is a forest.

Only few take lessons from the tragedy of others.

Only in the gallery of education can a nation's future be carved out.

Opportunity is the lift to greatness.

Our compassion to one another makes us wholly human.

Our conscience is put to task when it is time to tell ourselves the truth.

Our dreams die when we can't wake up for it.

Our expiry date is our day with fate.

Our footprint on earth is the lives we touch and the hearts we hurt.

Our imperfections makes our perfectly human.

Our Life has a meaning, our death have a purpose.

Our life is a phase and so are our troubles.

Our life is a phase and so are our troubles.

Our lives are ruled by our circumstance, our choices, our fate.

Our responsibility tracks our mind.

Our spiritual significance makes no meaning without our moral significance.

Overload in life affects its speed.

Passion can plant a tree, patient nurtures it.

Pay your rent regularly and never fail to greet her every morning, that' s the law of the Landlady.

People not good in keeping the secrets of others secret, are good in keeping their own.

People who can't find success find a blame.

People who don't dance in the public, dance when they are alone.

People who write books have no lifespan.

People with limited needs have limited problems and limited progress.

Periodically free your brain and mind of excess load, to make room for new entries.

Physical forces subdues, moral force wins.

Plucking a coconut is not the same as plucking a paw paw.

Practices give life to principles.

Proximity makes good and bad accessible and achievable.

Pursuit of a good job is pursuit of happiness. Having a good job is pursuit of happiness.

Real estate doesn't mean there's a fake one.

Reasoning restricts passion.

Responsibility is taking responsibility.

Running stomach leads to running legs.

Science explains life and create none.

Science needs mathematics, Life needs Arithmetic.

Scriptures and money are seriously competing for the Hearts of men.

Seeing the dawn is the first gift of the day.

Self harmstems from self indulgence.

Share your sorrow with your friends and your joy with everyone.

Sleep on speed and slip away.

Some clothes in a congested wardrobe will never be worn.

Some of our problems are simply waiting for our decisions.

Some secrets when revealed, shatters lives forever.

Some words come with flames, some with water.

Someday, somewhere, somehow, everyone will breath his last.

Someday, somewhere, somehow, everyone will breath his last.

Stolen goods are sold at low prices

Straight road encourages deadly speed.

Success in life begins with great ideas and follow them through.

Success is in the will to succeed.

Suicide is of the weak without the courage to live.

Tell your friend a fake secret before the real one.

Temptation wins over a weak soul.

Tenancy is tyranny.

The acts of the morning are the thoughts of the Night.

The advice given to children is not necessary the advice headed by parents.

The aging spirit gets wiser in a body getting weaker.

The belief that you can overcome, makes you an overcomer.

The best advice comes from persons who have been in trouble.

The best of all dishes can't be eaten with a troubled mind.

The best of friend is present when you are absent.

The brain only stores what attention transmits to it.

The call room of the Lord is busier in times of distress.

The calmness of the old man is an experience from a hurry.

The death of a Lion is confirmed with a stone, not a stick.

The demise of one industry is the rise of another.

The Earth can provide for our needs, not our greed.

The Earth can provide for our needs, not our greed.

The evil of man makes mortality the only means of continuity.

The fear of a new year are its contents, the hope of a new year are its promises.

The fears of the young is life and of the old is death.

The future is that we are uncertain but hopeful.

The god of the mind has the largest of followers.

The Gold you give out endures more than the Gold you stock.

The Grave is a lift.

The greatness of a son comes at the twilight of the father.

The greatness of God is in the triumph of justice and the mystery of death.

The Hands of a blind beggar can differentiate currency denominations.

The heart can take you to the desert or the river.

The heart has no compass.

The hungry is entertained with food, not with music.

The key to happiness in troubling times is holding to the belief that everything lives a phase.

The Lantern glows in the absence of the Sun.

The lessons of death fades with the grief.

The life you live, the legacy you leave.

The limitation of a fat bank account is that it won't add a second to your life.

The little insult you ignore is a test for a big one.

The little insult you ignore is a test for a big one.

The longest journey is the one you have not started.

The Lord reaches where the Law cant.

The Lord reaches where the Law cant.

The lot of your fears, the lot of your chains.

The milk of human kindness can never be split.

The mind reaches the destination before the body begins the journey.

The moment you own is the moment you live.

The most meanest of murderers is the killer of children.

The Neck can bear the Head and a load not more than the head.

The only echo from your grave is the echo of your legacy.

The only habit you can change after age forty is the eating habit.

The past is changed by a confession, the future is shaped by a resolve.

The patient earth takes our fury and our body.

The poor attend to their worries in voices, the Rich attend to their worries in silence.

The poor's wardrobe reveals his capacity, the rich wardrobe reveals his taste.

The power of faith is in the power of its truth.

The pretty face behind the counter may be sitting on a wheel chair.

The problem of those who have choices is choice, the problem of those without choice is choices.

The pyramid of stolen money is eaten by termites.

The quality of contents of a refuse dumb is the quality of life of the people in its location.

The quality of your faith is the quality of your morality.

The rich and the poor go to the grave on hired vehicle.

The same Sun that blossom the beautiful Rose also withers if away.

The shoes tells about the day, the Bed sheet about the night.

The shoes tells about the day, the Bedsheet about the night.

The significance of the father makes surname first.

The soul cannot be cremated.

The Tongue and the Hand are the outlets of anger.

The tragedy of others shocks more and teaches less.

The train of confusion never arrives at a decision.

The trophy of success is hidden in the forest of disappointments.

The trouble with life is that it is attached to troubles.

The truth needs no audit if it's the truth.

The two fingers that can snap, have been approved from creation.

The venerability of a python is in its food.

The weight of a handcuff is heavier than its metal.

The weight of a Handcuff is heavier than its metallic substance.

The will of the dead depends on the compliance of the living.

The world is an old fabric, when one part is sown, another part is torn.

The world is too busy to remember an expensive wedding.

The world of children is a world of fantasy.

There are moments one doesn't like making progress, when one reaches a cliff.

There are some tragedies beyond the flow of tears.

There's joy in winning, there's lesson in loosing.

There is a rain beyond an umbrella.

There is a truth reserved only for the dead.

There is no better future other than the one you work for it.

There is no distance a mind cannot cover.

There is no eloquence like the truth.

There is no night life where there is no day life.

There is no premature death, every life has a span.

There is no rush hour in the village.

There is nothing as fast as the dateline for debt and rent payment.

Thievery needs a market.

Thorough the rock and sands is to the diamond.

Those above vanity are above want.

Those fruits not eaten at homes are eaten in the clinic.

Those things the children destroyed in the house, are the building blocks of the house.

Those who ascribe massive wealth of a few to the Lord ascribes massive poverty of the many to the Lord.

Those who compassionately visit you in prison will prayerfully visit your grave.

Those who compassionately visit you in prison, will prayerfully visit your grave.

Those who eat Bad beans have lose their right to remain silent.

Those who eat Bad beans have lose their right to remain silent.

Those who made it at old age, try to make up.

Time rescues a widow from the chains of grief.

To agree to be loved is to agree to a journey.

To aim higher, you must pull the catapult string harder.

To control your mind is to control your world.

To die young is to miss the joy of old age, and the burden of it.

To die young is to rot early in life.

To fly to the top, you must overcome the pull of gravity.

To give is not to have but to believe in giving.

To know little is not to know nothing. To know much is not to know all.

To know more about your home, you need to go out of your home.

To live long is a wish, to live forever is a mirage.

To live long is to experience the sorrows of later life.

To read a book, you need silence. To live the book, you need the noise.

To speak diplomatically is to dilute your truth.

To succeed in Life, you need a spirit of possibilities.

To survive, adapt to change, to excel, lead the change.

To the hungry, food is Gold.

To wake up in the morning is to unwrap the package of the day.

To worship, you must first be free to worship.

Treasure every moment with your parents, they will only be with you for a while.

Truth is the best of eloquence.

Trying moments is your moment of trial.

Turbulent waves ignites fervent prayer.

Uncertainty leads to diversification.

Unlike goat head pepper soup, words of wisdom needs deeper thoughts.

Vanities either bid you bye or you bid them bye.

We all have fears in life, but some can overcome them better.

We build our lives on the foundation of our dreams.

We came from the unknown to live in the known and disappear to the unknown.

We come to the world unblemished and depart with spots of our deeds.

We die because we are meant to die.

We die in each sleep to die forever.

We hold true to our beliefs in the hope that our belief is the truth.

We live in a small world but exist in a big one.

We live life as something and end it as nothing.

We live once in life and ever in memory.

We live our life in the lives of others.

We live our times and leave in others times.

We need God because man is more controlled by mystery.

We need God because man is more controlled by mystery.

What controls the mind controls the body.

What you need to live is average, what you need to waste is much.

What you say is the body of your word, what you mean is the soul.

Whatever is happening here had happened somewhere and will happen elsewhere.

Whatever rule your soul, rules your body.

When a bush fire rages, snakes and rats have no time for malice.

When a child is killed, a bridge is burnt.

When a creditor visits a debtor, he gets special courtesy.

When a man dies, his credit and debts comes alive.

When a Man is on a Tower, he sees everyone faintly and everyone sees him faintly.

When a rabbit is running towards the hunter, it is chased by a python.

When a snake climbs a tree, the monkey does not make territorial claims.

When a Tiger has nothing to eat, it eats its master.

When all know what to be said, none will like to stay.

When all parents are dead, there's nowhere to run to but the scriptures.

When all parents are dead, there's nowhere to run to but the scriptures.

When all your contemporaries are gone, you don't need a clock to know it is time.

When chopping down a Tree, the side you stand matters.

When dead, you are through with friends and foes.

When death takes away our loved ones from our eyes, it keeps them in our Heart for the rest of our lives.

When different people live together, the ambience is a school.

When in prison, never provoke a Life time serving inmate, he has nothing to lose.

When in prison, never provoke a Life time serving inmate, he has nothing to lose.

When in the cell, you will learn to live with those you think you can't.

When it rains heavily, you don't need a faith to walk on water.

When it rains heavily, you don't need a faith to walk on water.

When many unimportant things occupy your mind, there will be no space for few important things.

When one succeeds, some get inspired, some get envious.

When others determine your happiness, they will determine your sorrow.

When poor people are happy, it amazes the rich.

When tasting a new food, it pauses on the tongue for a while.

When the love of others rules your life, the life of others is your soul.

When the mouth tells lies about age, the body counters with the truth.

When the only river is infested with crocodiles, monkeys prefer to lick the morning dew.

When the soul is out of the body, the body becomes an object.

When there are too many deaths, there is too little time for mourning.

When we are gone, no matter how long we are remembered, we will still be long forgotten.

When worshipers pray to God and watching the window, the Satan is lurking around.

When you are younger, there things you can't see, when older, there are things you can't say.

When you buy what you don't need, you will sell it at auction.

When you change your curtains, you get a new ray, new breeze, new spirit through your window.

When you count your Blessings in vanity, you have no blessing.

When you give up, you have given in.

When you go to an event with a borrowed wrapper, avoid quarrels.

When you gossip a lot, you lose the intelligence to discuss issues.

When you have a flying determination, you can't be limited by a cliff.

When you have an hour to speak about what u know, don't just fill up the time with what you don't know.

When you have no goals in life, you will have no goalpost.

When you know you are on the right path, only look at the road signs.

When you light up the dark, you create a path.

When you live by envy, you will die by anguish.

When you live long in the world, you become a stranger.

When you live long, you find yourself in a world different from the one you knew.

When you lose hope about life, you are as good as been dead.

When you lose hope, you have no arsenal left.

When you make a promise, your integrity is on the gallows, when u fulfill it, its rescued.

When you plant a tree of kindness, your grave will be under its shade.

When you reach a cross road, ponder all routes.

When you stand atop the mountain of fame, you then have to contend with the wind.

When you wear a white cloth, people will be looking for a sign of stain.

When you wrestle a madman, make sure he doesn't pull off your clothes.

When your life is in tatters, you are the best of all tailors to sew it back.

When your needs are limited, so will be your woes.

Whereas the rich needs drugs to sleep, the poor just need food to sleep.

Whereas the rich needs drugs to sleep, the poor just need food to sleep.

White skin glow best in a Black fabric.

Wisdom like arts needs deeper understanding.

Women make up with creams, men make up with herbs.

Women who slap housemaids, don't expect retaliation.

Women's advice will take you away from harm and away from progress.

Women's' advice will take you away from harm and away from progress.

Wrinkles denote kilometers covered.

You are born on the ground, you rise above ground and end underground.

You can accurately chose where to live but not accurately where to die.

You can be a prisoner of your indecision.

You can be alive without living a life.

You can be born with a silver spoon, but you must learn table manners.

You can be rich and become honest but you can't be honest and become rich.

You can buy a Title but not a honour.

You can confront your problems or submit to it.

You can detach yourself from reality but not from your conscience.

You can fake your age, not your agility.

You can have a contest of beauty but not of morals.

You can know most things but not all things about your partner.

You can lead a horse to the river but you can't force it to drink, not when you have more distance to cover.

You can live a life without knowing the world.

You can neither predict God nor the mind of a Human being.

You can never graduate from the school of Life.

You can own the world but must leave it behind.

You can run away from your problems to meet it at your destination.

You can't be fed and be honoured.

You can't build a perfect home from a distance.

You can't enjoy a good music with a troubled mind.

You can't fly over your problems and arrive at a solution.

You can't fly over your problems and arrive at a solution.

You can't quench a thirst with a cream of gold.

You can't read a book without a reading habit.

You can't spit on a man and dictate to him on how to react.

You can't throw a stone afar with a closed armpit.

You cannot bend safe and on speed.

You cannot cut the prison bar in a day.

You cannot tile the rough surface of reality.

You can't always win in life because failure also has a queue.

You can't escape death, it's just not your time.

You can't excel if all you do is what all are doing.

You can't master life, you will die learning.

You control your mind, you control the devil.

You don't aim once at a mango with a stone and give up because you missed it.

You don't know trouble if you have never been in trouble.

You don't need a religion to do good, you need a religion to avoid evil.

You don't need much to live much.

You dream on a pillow of stones.

You must be a successful at present for your past to matter.

You must travel or mix widely to have a broader perspective of life.

You need to be deserted by friends once in your life, to clear yourself of doubt.

You should slow down for a bump to save the car.

You wish to be somebody, somebody wishes to be you.

You won't know much about height when rising in a lift.

Your beliefs are your gods.

Your body cannot belong to where your soul does not belong.

Your future is someone else past and someone else present.

Your future is tomorrow but your time is now.

Your problems holds a gun, to patiently await the arrival of your money.

Your sustenance is attach to your beliefs.

Revolution

Poverty leads to revolt or to submission.

The happy children of looters will share a world with the angry children of the looted.

Education

A child walking to the school is a child walking to the future.

An exam only grades retentive memory, not intelligence.

As long as a public officials do not patronize public schools, so shall it remain a public embarrassment.

Geniuses have no label, a nation must provide opportunities for all.

Geniuses have no label, a nation must provide opportunities for all.

If a child is denied knowledge in the class, he will get it in the street.

In a class, some students will be Bankers, some depositors, some Robbers.

In the class, all students face one direction, in Life they face different.

It is for the peace of the children of the rich, for the children of the poor to be well educated.

Learning is light, ignorance is darkness.

Most free education classes are free of furniture.

Most pharmacists wanted to be Doctors.

No nation can grow beyond its education status.

Public schools and public toilets have a lot in common.

Public schools, bad schools, good polling centers.

Rebellious ideas advances the frontiers of knowledge.

The mind of a child is blank and magnetizing.

The quality of our students, the quality of our future.

The school is about the student, the class is about the teacher.

The street accepts whom the school rejects.

To read a book, you have to cut off from the world, to live the Bank, you have to cut off from the book.

Waste of opportunity is worse than a waste of time.

We are in a new world that probes our intelligence daily.

What the gym is for the body is what the library is for the brain.

When menial jobs caught up with the Ph.Ds, next is the professors.

When students learn under trees, they become shadow learners.

When you read, you are up loading, when you write, you are down loading.

You can kill people for being different from you but that can never make them you.

Business

Bankers keep their hearts at home when recovering a loan.